Illustrator:
José L. Tapia

Editor:
Walter Kelly, M.A.

Editorial Project Manager:
Karen Goldfluss, M.S. Ed.

Editor-in-Chief:
Sharon Coan, M.S. Ed.

Art Director:
Elayne Roberts

Associate Designer:
Denise Bauer

Cover Artist:
Larry Bauer

Production Manager:
Phil Garcia

Imaging:
Hillary Merriman

Publishers:
Rachelle Cracchiolo, M.S. Ed.
Mary Dupuy Smith, M.S. Ed.

April
Monthly Activities

Intermediate

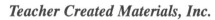
Author:
Dona Herweck Rice

Teacher Created Materials, Inc.
P.O. Box 1040
Huntington Beach, CA   92647
ISBN-1-55734-877-4

©*1995 Teacher Created Materials, Inc.*   Made in U.S.A.

Table of Contents

Teacher Information 3

April Calendar and Events 6

Seasonal Activities...8

    April Holidays and Special Events 8

    April Personalities 33

    April Showers 44

    Earth Day 55

Management Pages 64

Answer Key 80

Introduction

The monthly activity books in this series have been created specifically for the intermediate level. The activities within the books are meant to enhance your current curriculum with supporting seasonal themes. You may choose just those activities that work best for you or use the activities in total. The introductory teacher pages included at the start of each book will provide any information needed in addition to the activity pages themselves.

A variety of management pages have also been included to support the seasonal atmosphere of your classroom. These pages include open worksheets and worksheet ideas, a record form, an invitation, a thank you note, a contract, an award, a news page for parents or absentee students, a parent request letter, seasonal clip art, stationery, and a bulletin board complete with any necessary patterns.

Teacher Information

Easter (pages 8–11): The first three activities on these pages have the students explore some traditional and commercial elements of Easter, eggs, baskets, and Easter hats. Page 11 requires that they do some research to discover the roots of Easter. They should be able to find the information on their own, particularly in small groups if they have access to a library or if a variety of reference books are brought into the classroom. In the paragraphs below is some information that may help.

Easter Sunday is considered one of the holiest in the Christian year because it celebrates the resurrection of Jesus Christ. *Resurrection* means that he rose from the dead. Easter may have first come to be celebrated in the spring because of its message of life and rebirth. Also, the early Christian church often placed its holy days in conjunction with pagan festivals, and early spring has long been a common time for celebrating.

The name *Easter* may be derived from Eostre, the Roman goddess of spring and fertility. The goddess favored the hare, and this may be the origin of the Easter bunny. However, the Easter bunny does not deliver eggs in all countries around the world. The French say that the eggs are brought by the ringing of church bells, and elsewhere in the world they are thought to be delivered by foxes, doves, or cranes.

The day on which Easter is celebrated rotates from March 22 through April 21, depending on the Christian calendar. However, it is always celebrated on the first Sunday after the first full moon after the vernal equinox. Therefore, from 1996 through the year 2000, Easter falls on April 7, March 30, April 12, April 4, and April 23, respectively.

Passover (pages 12–13): These two pages deal with the Seder, the opening meal of the eight-day Jewish holiday. You may wish to give the students additional information about the holiday, and you can do so by offering in your classroom library both fiction and nonfiction books that deal with the subject. You may also read the story of the Exodus to the class and perhaps show them a

film version of the story as done in one of the many Hollywood epics on this Biblical subject.

Also, let the students know that the celebration of Passover falls somewhere in March or April, varying from year to year. This is due to the Jewish calendar which is lunisolar (meaning its year is measured by the sun, and the months are measured by the moon). From 1996 through the year 2000, Passover begins on April 7, April 22, April 11, April 1, and April 20, respectively.

April Fool's Day (pages 14–17): These four pages include three diverting activities that are in keeping with the day, as well as one thought-provoking activity that considers both the historic and modern role of the fool.

Library Week (page 18): This page centers on the Dewey Decimal System, and it can be done individually or in pairs. You may wish to tour the school library while discussing the Dewey Decimal System. You may also wish to give the students the following additional information at the point indicated on page 18:

Where in the 500's depends on additional factors. These are the books' division and section. (For example, 560 marks the division and 568 marks the section). This number can be followed by one or more subsections that are placed after a decimal (for example, 568.64). The entire number, including the subsections, is called the book's *class number.*

A class number will often be followed on the next line by a *call number* which contains the first letter of the author's last name. It might also include a *cutter number* which is determined by the librarian for help in organizing and shelving the books. Finally, it might include the first letter of the title, excluding *the, a,* and *an.*

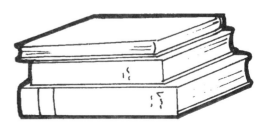

Teacher Information (cont.)

International Children's Book Day (page 19):
As a class, have the students name some of their favorite books now and when they were younger. Also name some of your favorite childhood books. Write these titles on the board or an overhead. Leave the titles up as the students do the activity on page 19. You may have to help some children who do not have much experience with books by helping them recall stories they remember or stories you have read in class.

To further support the meaning of the day, build or add to your classroom library. Focus on books from or about cultures around the world. Share some special books with the students. Ask parents to donate some appropriate books, perhaps even their childhood favorites.

World Health Day (pages 20–21): Enlarge the patterns from page 21 and place them in a vertical column on the left edge of a large sheet of butcher paper. Next to each pattern, write the students' ideas from page 20 for healthy bodies, minds, and hearts. Let the students color healthy and happy images (people, animals, plant life, etc.) around the perimeter of the paper. Display the poster in your classroom or school.

Hana Matsuri (page 22): *Hana Matsuri*, April 8, marks Buddha's birthday. To celebrate the Zen Buddhist tradition, the students are shown two Zen haiku. They are then asked to create their own.

Arbor Day (pages 23–24): Two activities are offered for Arbor Day, which usually falls in April but is celebrated on different days throughout the United States and the world. It was first celebrated on April 10, 1872.

On page 23, the students are asked "to make" a class tree. This is a whole-class project. Then, on page 24, they will brainstorm in small groups for the many uses of trees. It is suggested that, as a class, they plant a tree in honor of Arbor Day and as a reminder to replenish the resources we use.

Barbershop Quartet Day (page 25): Though barbershop quartets had their greatest popularity many years ago, there are barbershop quartets performing today. If possible, take a field trip to see a quartet perform or invite a quartet to your school. Many quartets use humor as a part of their act, so the students will have an additional reason for enjoying the performance.

To extend the activity on page 25, which has the students name things that come in fours, ask the students if they can think of any modern popular quartets that blend harmonies as the key to their performances. There are several such groups on the popular music charts today.

Solar New Year (page 26): Before doing the activity on this page, discuss the concept of culture with the students. Brainstorm with them for some local cultural customs. Share with them the customs of your culture.

Sports and Fitness Day (page 27): The class is asked to create an obstacle course. Each participant is given an award certificate. You might wish to do this activity together with the activity on pages 20 and 21 for World Health Day.

Make a Quilt Day (page 28): The students are instructed to create their own quilt squares from colored paper. If you wish to provide them with examples, offer those shown. You can enlarge them or show them on the overhead projector.

Goodwill Day (pages 29–30): Goodwill Day is celebrated in the United States and Canada on April 23. It celebrates the goodwill between the two nations. If you are citizens of the United States, have the students use the form on page 29. If you are citizens of Canada, have the students use the form on page 30. On their form they should write five positive things that they know about the country on the page. If research is needed, provide the appropriate reference books.

Teacher Information (cont.)

Auto Licenses (page 31): The students will decode and create personalized license plates. To extend this, you might challenge them by asking them to create plates for specific occupations or hobbies, such as a doctor, a teacher, rock climbing, etc.

National Humor Month (page 32): A variety of class and individual activities are suggested. To extend, show the students a classic movie or two, such as those starring Laurel and Hardy, Buster Keaton, or the Marx Brothers. They are likely to be surprised at how much they enjoy them.

Maya Angelou (page 33): The students are asked to write a poem that conveys Angelou's love and respect for people. As an extension, read some of her poems or excerpts from her books. Some of her poems are published as children's picture books.

Betty Ford/First Ladies (pages 34–35): To extend either of the two activities on these pages, ask the students to consider and write about their personal agendas if they were to become First Lady or First Gentleman.

Thomas Jefferson (page 36): The puzzle on this page provides a variety of the roles played by Thomas Jefferson. To extend, have student teams research the specifics of one of the roles.

Anne Sullivan Macy (page 37): There is much more to sign language than the alphabet. Have the students research sign languages, perhaps even learning a few words and phrases.

Leonardo da Vinci (page 38): Before developing their own flying machines, you may wish to have the students learn something of aeronautics.

Friedrich Froebel (page 39): As the students share their kindergarten memories, also share yours. Invite parents to share their stories with the students as well.

William Shakespeare (pages 40–41): For a challenging extension after producing their own plays, have the students work in teams to reproduce either a model of the Globe Theater or an Elizabethan costume (doll size).

James Audubon (page 42): After completing this activity, have the students research the Audubon Society and learn about its mission.

Coretta Scott King (page 43): As an extension, ask the students to find the titles of books on the Coretta Scott King Award list. Learn about the award and why it is given. Share some of the books with the class.

April Showers (pages 44–54): The activities on these pages have something to do with rain. They include word games (pages 48, 51, and 52), arts and crafts (pages 44, 49, and 50), a just-for-fun game page (54), and science pages that involve the water cycle (pages 45 and 46) and rainfall around the world (page 53). Page 46 should be used in conjunction with page 45, testing the students on what they have learned. It is also a test in logical sequencing.

Earth Day (pages 55–63): All of these pages are centered around Earth Day and are environmental in nature. Pages 55 and 56 are meant as take-home projects. Duplicate the cards and pass them out to the students at random. Ask them to complete any three in a row on their cards. When complete, you can reward each student with a prize or the certificate on page 69.

Students can practice their own recycling with the activities on pages 57, 59, and 60. On page 58 they will take an ecology survey. Administer this survey before your Earth Day unit and again afterwards. Discuss any changes in their responses. Page 61 offers a recipe for rock candy, a fun way to enjoy the "earth." This is followed by writing topics on page 62. These can be done in journals, in cooperative groups, or as more formal, individual writing activities. The final page, 63, offers a word puzzle dealing with the products of the rain forest. To extend, investigate the rain forest with your students and have them discover how it is threatened. Discuss ways that they can make a difference in halting the deforestation.

April

Sunday	Monday	Tuesday	Wednesday	Thursday	Friday	Saturday

April Events

The following events and holidays take place in the month of April. Have the students complete the calendar (page 6) by putting the 30 dates of April in their appropriate places and by adding the events or holidays listed below that you would like to include. (You may need to determine the holiday dates for the current year.) Also include the April birthdays of students in your classroom. Finally, the students may use this calendar as a record for their homework during the month.

- **Easter** (Christian, rotates between March 22 and April 21)
- **Passover** (Jewish, varies each year, either in March or April)
- **April Fool's Day** (April 1)
- **Library Week** (U.S.A., first week of April; first American public library opened April 9, 1833)
- **International Children's Book Day** (April 2)
- **Birth of Maya Angelou** (April 5, 1928)
- **World Health Day** (April 7)
- **Hana Matsuri** (Buddhist, Buddha's Birthday, April 8)
- **Birth of Betty Ford** (April 8, 1918)
- **Arbor Day** (first celebrated April 10, 1872; date varies internationally)
- **Barbershop Quartet Day** (U.S.A., April 11)
- **Birth of Thomas Jefferson** (April 13, 1743)
- **Birth of Anne Sullivan Macy** (April 13, 1886)
- **Solar New Year** (Asian, April 13 or 14)
- **Birth of Leonardo da Vinci** (April 15, 1452)
- **Sports and Fitness Day** (U.S.A., April 17)
- **Make a Quilt Day** (U.S.A., April 20)
- **Birth of Friedrich Froebel** (April 21, 1782)
- **Earth Day** (April 22)
- **Goodwill Day** (Canada and U.S.A., April 23)
- **Birth of William Shakespeare** (probably April 23, 1564)
- **Birth of Ella Fitzgerald** (April 25, 1918)
- **First automobile license issued** (April 25, 1901)
- **Birth of James Audubon** (April 26, 1785)
- **Birth of Coretta Scott King** (April 28, 1927)
- **National Humor Month** (U.S.A.)

Easter Egg

Easter is an ancient Christian holiday that celebrates the resurrection of Jesus Christ. It is celebrated around the world on the first Sunday after the first full moon of spring. That day falls anywhere from March 22 through April 21.

However, Easter is not solely a Christian holiday. Today it is commonly observed commercially with Easter eggs, baskets of candy, the Easter Bunny, and new clothes and festive hats.

Traditional Easter eggs are hardboiled and then decorated with vinegar and water dyes. To make more vibrant and lasting eggs, follow these directions:

Materials:

- egg
- utensil with a sharp, pointed tip
- bowl
- water
- acrylic paints
- paintbrushes

Directions:

1. Have an adult gently poke through the shell of the egg with the pointed instrument at the top and the bottom of the egg. Ask him or her to be careful to make only two small holes and no additional cracks.
2. Hold the egg over the bowl, and placing your lips over the hole on one end, blow gently. This should slowly push the yolk and white of the egg through the other hole and into the bowl. Set the yolk and white aside and use them later for cooking.
3. Gently rinse the shell in water, inside and out. Let it dry.
4. Carefully paint any picture or design you would like on the shell of the egg. Let it dry.
5. Display your egg on a stand or in a basket.

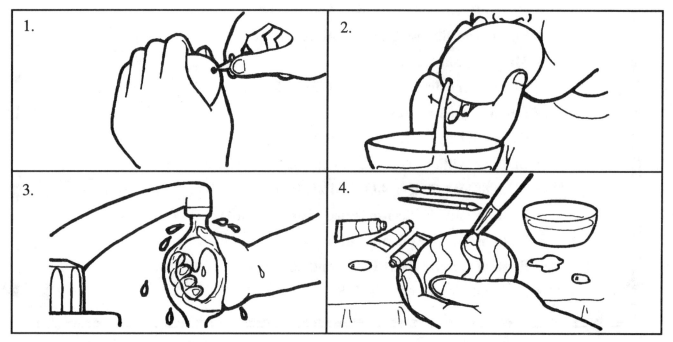

Easter Basket

Easter baskets are traditionally said to be delivered by the Easter bunny early Easter morning. They are filled with such things as decorated eggs, chocolate bunnies, chocolate chicks, and artificial grass. Each of the items placed in the basket is supposed to be a symbol for new life because Easter itself represents the resurrection of life.

What symbolizes or represents life for you? Think about that and write your ideas on the back of this paper. Then, in the Easter basket below, draw or write the most important five things that symbolize life for you.

Easter Hat

The Easter hat or bonnet is a favorite tradition of Easter. Traditionally, women, men, and children purchase or make new hats to be worn for the first time on Easter day. They wear the hats to church or, as seen in the classic film by that name, to the Easter Parade. The hats are usually decorative and festive, often bedecked with flowers and ribbons.

Using any materials you have or can find, such as construction paper, fabric, newspaper, ribbons, tissue paper, and so forth, make and decorate an Easter hat. Hold a class contest to choose the best hats in various categories, such as the most colorful, most imaginative, or all-around best.

Easter History

What do you know about the history of Easter? In the space below, list five facts that have to do with the origin of Easter and its traditions. For example, why is Easter celebrated? Who celebrates it? Where does the word *Easter* come from? Where does the story of the Easter bunny originate? Use these and/or additional questions. When your work is complete, share your findings with the class.

Teacher Note: See page 3.

Passover

Passover is an eight-day Jewish holiday that commemorates the deliverance of the Hebrews from slavery in Egypt over 3,000 years ago. The story can be read in the Jewish book called Haggadah or in the Bible in the book of Exodus. (Teacher note: See page 3.)

The celebration of Passover begins with a special meal called the Seder. Each food on the Seder plate, which is placed in the center of the table, has symbolic significance.

Using logic and, perhaps, prior knowledge, draw lines matching each food on the Seder plate to the thing it is likely to represent. Take your best guess. Your teacher has the answers and will tell you how well you matched the items.

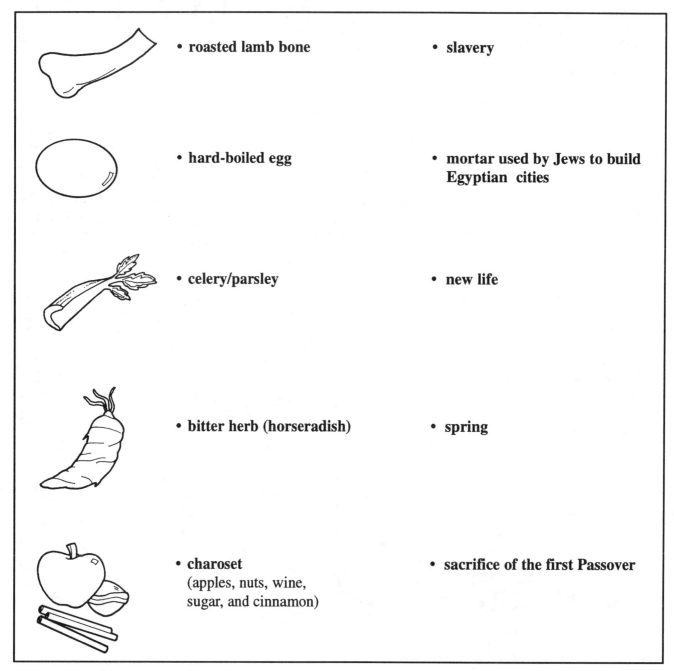

Passover

Make a Seder plate to learn about the Passover symbols. Color the plate below and cut it out. Then cut along the bold lines. Next, cut a circle the same size as the Seder plate out of a separate sheet of paper. Attach the center of the two circles (with the Seder plate on top) with glue or a brass fastener. Finally, lift each section of the Seder plate and on the paper under it, write a brief description of the food that is pictured and what it symbolizes.

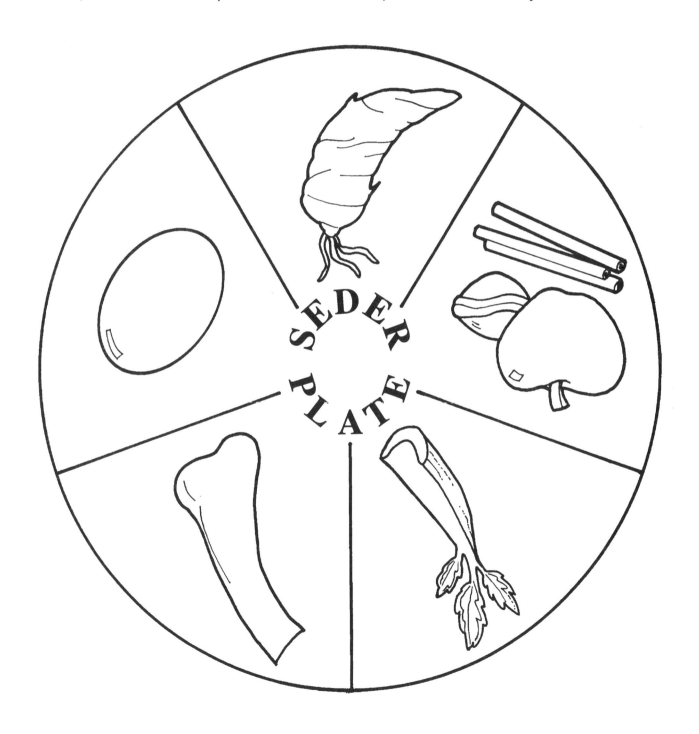

April Fool's Day

What would an April Fool be without a fool's hat? Follow these directions to construct a hat from newspapers. Then, decorate it as desired.

Materials:

- old newspapers
- paper and fabric scraps
- scissors
- buttons, sequins, beads, package bows, yarn, and ribbons in various colors

- paints and paintbrushes
- crayons and markers
- glue
- clear tape

Directions:

1. Cut or tape the paper (depending on its current size) to make a rectangle of approximately 22" x 17" (56 cm x 43 cm).

2. Fold the paper in half along the 22" (56 cm) edge.

3. Fold the paper in half again, as shown.

4. Open the fold. Fold the top left and right corners down to meet at the center fold.

5. Fold up the bottom flap on this side and on the reverse side.

6. Pull the center front and the center back out and away from each other. Tuck one flap corner behind the other flap corner on both sides. You now have a diamond shape.

7. Fold the bottom two corners up one quarter of the entire length of the hat.

8. Pull the new center front and center back out and away from each other. You now have a pointed fool's hat with an octagonal (eight-sided) base.

9. Add cones and tubes made from rolled up newspapers to create the look of a traditional fool's hat. Paint and decorate as desired.

10. Wear your hats to celebrate April Fool's Day!

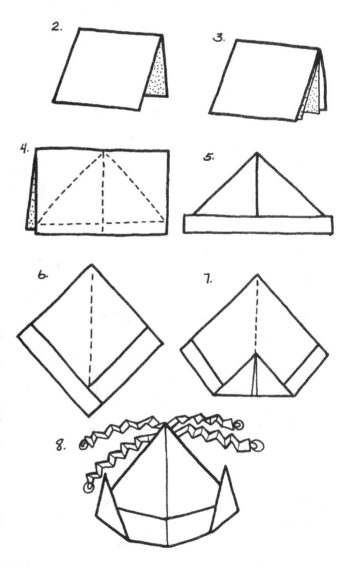

More April Fool's Day

The fools of history (and some people actually had that job!) were truly very clever and witty. Their function was to entertain the royalty. However, they had to be quite careful so as not to offend the king or queen, for if they did, their lives might have been at stake.

The playwright William Shakespeare usually portrayed the fools in his plays as the most insightful of all characters, those who best understood human nature and were able to point out the folly (silliness) of it.

Who in modern society plays the role of the fool such as Shakespeare described? Think about current comedians, public commentators, and even people you know personally. Choose one whom you think signifies a modern-day fool (in the classic sense!). Write about him or her here, explaining why you think that individual is like one of Shakespeare's fools.

_____

_____

_____

_____

_____

_____

_____

_____

_____

_____

_____

Still More April Fool's Day

Search the picture to find 20 things that are wrong.

A Final April Fool

This activity may or may not be appropriate for your school, but if the teacher determines that the climate is right, it will prove to be a great deal of fun.

In teams of three or four, brainstorm for several good-natured April Fool pranks that you can play on the principal, dean, or other top administrator of your school. Then, as a class (teacher, too!), share your ideas. Choose the best one and plan it out for April 1.

Brainstorm for your ideas here:

_____

_____

_____

_____

_____

_____

_____

_____

_____

_____

_____

_____

Make your plans on the back of this page.

Library Week

The first week of April is Library Week. It is a week to learn about, patronize, and be grateful for libraries. It is also a good time to start or add to your classroom or home library.

The traditional way in which books (excluding fiction and biographies) are classified in the library is by the Dewey Decimal System. This is a system of numbering books according to certain categories. See the chart below.

The 10 Dewey Decimal System Classes

000 - 099	Generalities	500 - 599	Pure Science
100 - 199	Philosophy	600 - 699	Technology
200 - 299	Religion	700 - 799	The Arts
300 - 399	Social Sciences	800 - 899	Language and Rhetoric
400 - 499	Language	900 - 999	Geography and History

Given this chart, a book entitled *Plant Life* will be given a 500 number. (Teacher: See page 3.)

Using the Dewey Decimal System, think of a real or imagined book title belonging to at least seven of the ten classes. However, the titles cannot be as simple as *A Book About Philosophy*, or *Religion for Beginners*. Use your creativity.

1. Generalities _____

2. Philosophy _____

3. Religion _____

4. Social Sciences _____

5. Language _____

6. Pure Science _____

7. Technology _____

8. The Arts _____

9. Language and Rhetoric _____

10. Geography and History _____

International Children's Book Day

April 2 is International Children's Book Day. To celebrate the day, choose one of your favorite books of all time and draw a memorable scene from that book. Write a brief description of the scene on the lines provided.

Title: _____

Author: _____

Scene: _____

_____

_____

_____

World Health Day

World Health Day is celebrated on April 7. It is a day for remembering the things a person needs to do in order to maintain a healthy body.

However, bodies are not the only part of being a healthy person. In the spaces below, write the things you can think of that are needed in order to have a healthy body, mind, and heart (emotions). When everyone has finished, share your ideas with the class. If you like some of the ideas given by other students, add them to your paper.

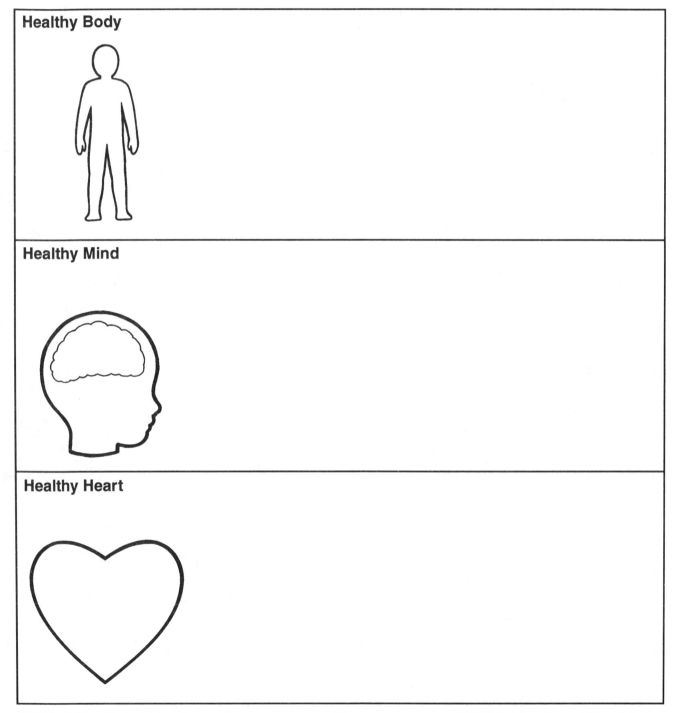

Healthy Body

Healthy Mind

Healthy Heart

"World Health Day" Patterns

Teacher: See page 4.

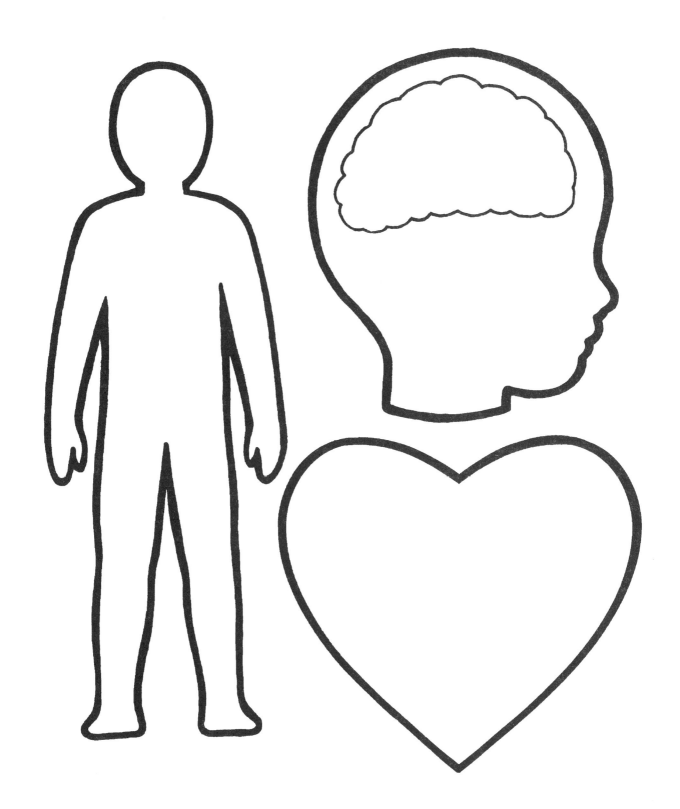

Hana Matsuri

The eighth day of April marks *Hana Matsuri*, the day that celebrates the birth, life, death, and enlightenment of Buddha, the originator of the Buddhist religion.

Buddhism is a religion that strongly supports peace and tranquility. An extension of Buddhism, particularly Zen Buddhism, is the popular (and tranquil) form of poetry known as haiku. Haiku first began as a 17-syllable stanza of poetry but later became a poem in itself. It is written in three lines, the first and third lines each having five syllables and the second line having seven.

Here are two ancient haiku. Please note that their syllable counts do not match because they have been translated from Japanese. Also included is a modern haiku.

Under cherry trees	May he who brings	April twilight pools
there are	flowers tonight,	shadows around a single
no strangers.	have moonlight.	rain-jeweled rosebud.
—Issa	—Kikaku	—Modern Haiku

Read over these haiku several times. On the lines below, construct your own. Remember, the message of the haiku should be a thoughtful and a peaceful one.

Arbor Day

Let the whole class join in a special project to celebrate Arbor Day. Follow these directions:

Materials:

- dead twigs and branches
- recycled paper
- green paint
- paint brushes
- wood glue
- string or hammer and nails (to be used with adult supervision)
- large pot
- dirt

Directions:

1. As a class, let the students construct a tree from the twigs and branches. They will join it with the glue, the string, or the hammer and nails.

2. Bed the "tree" in the pot with the dirt.

3. Add leaves to the tree by painting the paper green and cutting out leaf shapes. Glue them to the tree.

4. Throughout the week in which Arbor Day falls, display exceptional work or special art projects on the branches of your classroom tree. Of course, you might choose to display the tree through the remainder of your school year.

More Arbor Day

In teams of three or four, brainstorm the many uses of trees. When complete, come back together as a class and make a master list.

Now, in honor of Arbor Day, plant a tree on the school grounds. Dedicate it to the memory of your class. (Note: To earn money to purchase the tree, you can recycle paper and other recyclable materials.)

Barbershop Quartet Day

Barbershop Quartet Day is celebrated on April 11. A barbershop quartet is a specialized musical group of four which sings in harmony.

Can you think of anything else that comes in fours? Challenge yourself to list everything you can think of that comes in fours or is made of four parts.

Solar New Year

Solar New Year falls on April 13 or 14 in many Asian countries. It is called many things, including *Songkran* in Thailand, *Bun-Pi-Mai-Lao* in Laos, and *Baisakhi* in India. It is celebrated by cleansing of the old and preparing for the new. This is done symbolically by house cleaning, the kindling of new fires, new clothes being worn, and perhaps most festive, water thrown by the bucketful at people to bless them and wash away the troubles of the old year.

Of utmost importance to Southeast Asians who have moved to foreign countries is the passing on of their culture to their children. Cultural stories are told as part of the Solar New Year celebration.

If you were to have a Solar New Year celebration in your home, what stories might be told? What traditions might be shared? Choose one story or tradition and write it here. When everyone has finished, share it with the class.

_____

_____

_____

_____

_____

_____

_____

_____

_____

_____

_____

_____

_____

_____

Teacher note: See page 4.

Sports and Fitness Day

Sports and Fitness Day is April 17. To celebrate it, create an obstacle challenge course on your school playground. Prepare it as a class. Include such things as running in and out of cones, dribbling a basketball between two points, climbing across the monkey bars, and so forth. Time the students against one another or let them be a part of a team that gets timed together. When the challenge is complete, give each student a certificate of participation.

---

has completed the
Obstacle Challenge Course

Congratulations on your physical fitness!

signed

date

Make a Quilt Day

Quilting, though common many years ago, is a specialized art form today. That art is celebrated on Make a Quilt Day, April 20. Of course, this day is little known to most people, but you can honor it by designing a quilt square of your own.

Traditionally, quilts are made of pieces of fabric sewn in symmetrical designs in individual square sections, and then the squares are pieced together to form a large blanket. Everything together makes one big design.

To make a quilt square of your own, follow the directions below.

Materials:

- light colored paper
- dark colored paper
- patterned paper or an additional dark color
- ruler
- pencil
- scissors
- glue

Directions:

1. Cut the light paper to a 9" (22.5 cm) square.

2. Cut the dark paper to two 3" (7.5 cm) squares.

3. Cut the patterned or additional dark paper to two 3" (7.5 cm) squares.

4. Cut each of the 3" (7.5 cm) squares into two triangles. This is done evenly by drawing a line across the diagonal of each square, using the straight edge of the ruler from corner to corner.

5. Arrange the eight triangles you have made into a symmetrical design on the light square. When you are happy with your design, glue the triangles in place.

6. If desired, attach all the class squares together to make a class quilt. Display the quilt in your classroom or school.

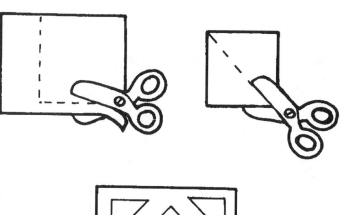

Alternative: Make the smaller squares 2" (5 cm). Make four of one and two of the other. You will then have eight triangles in one color and four in the other. Follow the rest of the directions above.

Goodwill Day

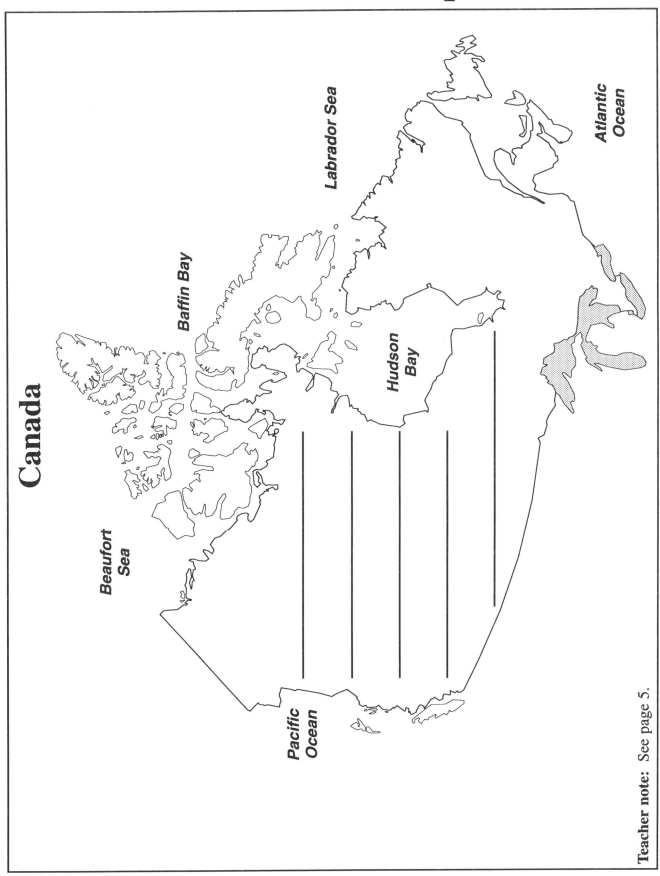

Goodwill Day (cont.)

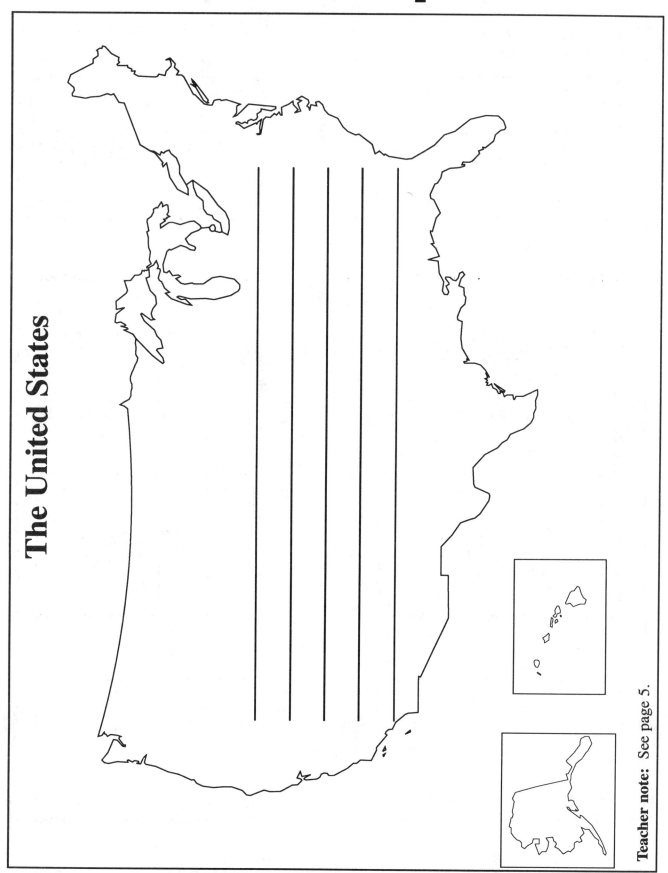

The United States

Teacher note: See page 5.

Auto Licenses

The first automobile license was issued on April 25, 1901. Today, personalized license plates are very popular. Can you interpret the plates below?

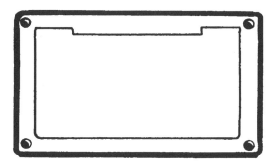

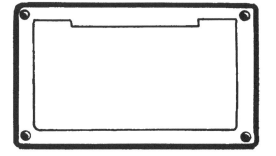

Now, create two plates of your own. Can others interpret your license plates?

National Humor Month

Class Activities

It's no joke—April is National Humor Month. Beginning with April Fool's Day, it is a month to giggle, smirk, and guffaw at all the humor life has to offer. To celebrate the month of humor, the class can do a variety of things. Below are a few ideas.

- Clip and display favorite comic strips.
- Collect jokes and put them in a class book.
- Make a newspaper comics page.
- Make an original joke book.
- Let those who dare try their hand at stand-up comedy.
- So, did you hear the one about . . . ?

Individual Activity

Use the form below to create original comics. The students can create their own unique strips, or you can challenge them by concealing the words of a printed comic strip and letting them write in their own.

Maya Angelou

The poet, writer, actress, producer, director, and activist, Maya Angelou, was born on April 5, 1928. She is perhaps best known for her novel *I Know Why the Caged Bird Sings.* She is also well known for the poem she was asked to write and read at President Clinton's inauguration in January of 1992.

Maya Angelou believes strongly in the worth and equality of all people. She treats everyone with great love and respect, and her work often reflects her beliefs.

As a tribute to Maya Angelou, write a poem that speaks positively about people. Share it with your teacher and a parent or friend. If you would like, share it with your class.

Betty Ford

Betty Ford, born April 8, 1918, is one of the United States' most respected former First Ladies. Her husband, Gerald Ford, was the president of the United States following the resignation of Richard Nixon. Mrs. Ford brought a great deal of awareness to the American people, particularly through her fight against breast cancer and her battle against alcoholism. She founded the world-renowned Betty Ford Clinic to help other alcoholics and addicts.

Though Betty Ford is best known for the above achievements, she also has another claim to fame. Her original desire was to be a dancer, and for awhile she was a member of Martha Graham's dance troupe, a prestigious group to which only the best could belong. She relinquished that dream for home and family, later to become First Lady and a true inspiration for her valiant struggles.

Betty Ford's first love and choice was to be a dancer, and though that was not her final career choice, she did accomplish that goal. In your heart of hearts, what is the thing that you would most like to do with your life? Write about it here. Also write about the steps you can take (and perhaps have taken) to make that dream a reality.

First Ladies

The First Ladies of the United States have traditionally taken causes to work for during their stays in the White House. They have often spoken to the public on these issues and sometimes pushed for legislation to make better the existing conditions.

Select one of the First Ladies named below. Do some research to discover what cause was closest to her heart. Also find out some basic information about her life, such as where and when she was born, the facts of her childhood, and her education and career.

Eleanor Roosevelt

Bess Truman

Mamie Eisenhower

Jacqueline Kennedy

Lady Bird Johnson

Pat Nixon

Rosalynn Carter

Nancy Reagan

Barbara Bush

Hillary Clinton

Thomas Jefferson

Thomas Jefferson was born on April 13, 1743. He was the president of the United States from 1801–1809, and he was also an accomplished inventor, farmer, architect, musician, and much more. Jefferson is commonly called a Renaissance Man, meaning he was a man able to do many things well.

Many of the things that Thomas Jefferson did in his lifetime can be found in the word puzzle below. There are ten of them. Can you find all ten? Your teacher has the answers if you need help.

```
K F J S S L X X H X W G T A M Y W P V D S P N S
D J M B D P Q C J P N S M R Q P F H R V T R J B
M J M Z D V Q B P R F X Q I W C C I G H A E S L
Z M U Z R L C D F L Y B R S P S W L X P T S N S
R H S N M G I V Y A M N P T T H Y O W X E I C G
W X I P Z L N N W W B F F O G B N S X F S D J P
C R C B N Y Y G V Y R K A C C G H O R Q M E Y J
V J I A R C H I T E C T G R F T C P M Q A N R M
D T A T V Y F K Q R N H V A M Y H H X Z N T M T
J X N K E T R G H D Q T R T P E W E F D N Y D Z
V H Z Z F R Y Q G S T X O V H Z R R N T N Z C S
M W Z M L S M Z Q X N B Z R S D V T C B P N T X
S H F Q Z Q H T R N F T C Y B K K W T G P K T B
Z C W B T Y S M R C G X Q X T J B Y C G V D S S
Z L C G Q C C Z C P F G G S N K T F M P K R L V
S F J N K B L K D H P T S K R S X K H M F Y T W
B D V J M Y T X B S N S B S N Q V N M X W V V
```

Anne Sullivan Macy

Anne Sullivan, born April 13, 1886, was the teacher and friend of Helen Keller, the blind and deaf girl who grew to be an accomplished woman and heralded orator. No one before had been able to teach Helen to communicate, but Anne did by spelling into Helen's hand with the sign language alphabet. She would form a letter in Anne's hands so that Anne could feel the shape of her hand and determine the letter.

Below is an illustration of the sign language alphabet. Together with a classmate, practice spelling words into one another's hands. Begin with two-letter words and then build from there. How well can you understand one another?

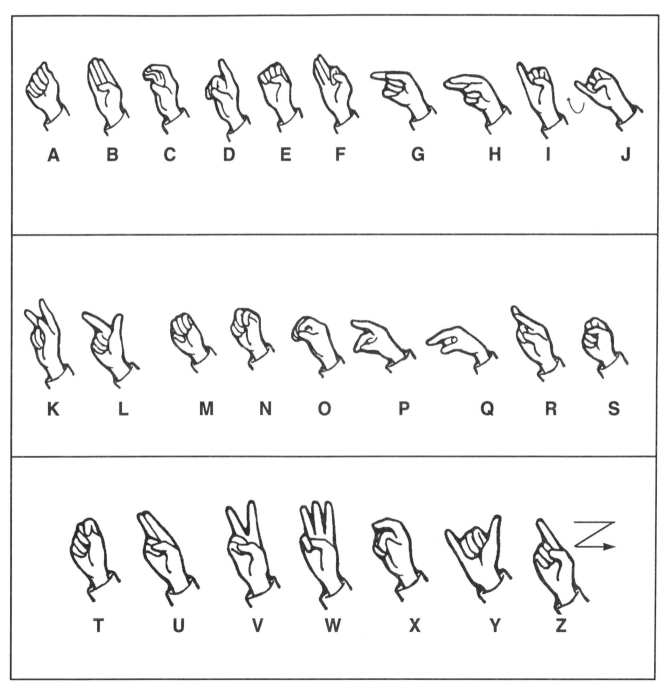

Leonardo da Vinci

Leonardo da Vinci was born on April 15, 1452. He was one of the world's most gifted artists, and his works, including the *Mona Lisa* and the *Last Supper*, are among the most famous of all time. However, Leonardo was not solely an artist. He was also a talented inventor. In fact, though he lived hundreds of years before functional airplanes came into being, he designed an airplane with amazing accuracy and foresight.

How well do you think you could design an airplane? Together in teams of three or four, design a model airplane or other flying machine out of paper, cardboard, fabric, or any materials you have available. You may not, however, make a simple paper airplane, and you may not use a design you already know or have found in a book or from a friend. Your team design must be original, and it must be able to fly for a minimum of five seconds.

The challenge has begun!

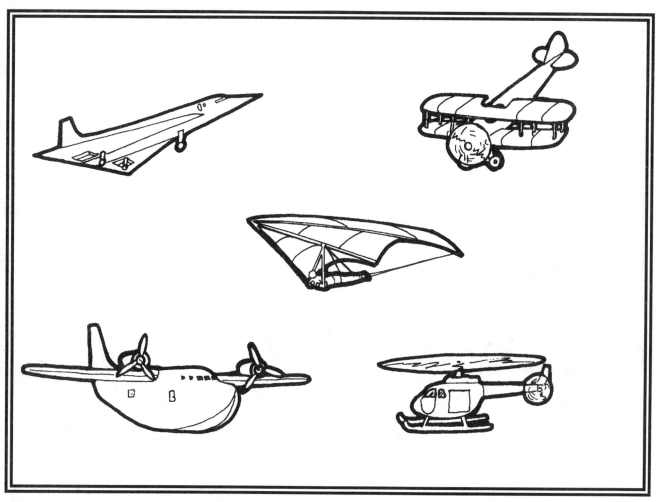

Friedrich Froebel

Friedrich Wilhelm August Froebel was a German educator who helped create the modern kindergarten. He was born on April 21, 1782.

Do you remember your year of kindergarten? Who was your teacher? What school did you attend? What did you learn? What games did you play?

In the space below, either write about a favorite kindergarten memory or draw a picture of it. In either case, give details.

William Shakespeare

William Shakespeare, perhaps the world's most famous poet and playwright, is known to have been born in April of 1564. He wrote and performed (for he was an actor as well) throughout the reign of Queen Elizabeth I, who died in 1603, and on into the reign of King James I. Shakespeare died in 1616.

Though the language of Shakespeare's writing is sometimes difficult for the modern reader to understand, once one understands its rhythms, it is among the most eloquent, humorous, and poignant of all writing. Moreover, Shakespeare's work is quite possibly the most enjoyable to see performed, for there is often a great deal of action, comical expression, or high drama evident in the performers.

To celebrate the life of William Shakespeare, have the students break into groups of four or five. Together, they will write a scene from a play, either an original one or a scene from a fairy tale, fable, or other story that they have never seen dramatized. Give them plenty of time to meet and write. Meet with each team to help them along and to approve their scripts. If desired, give them copies of the next page on which to write their final scripts.

Once written, have the teams rehearse their scenes. Be sure to structure this time with definite, measurable goals (such as the lines must be memorized by a certain time), or there is likely to be little productivity. When enough rehearsal time has been allowed, have the teams perform for the class.

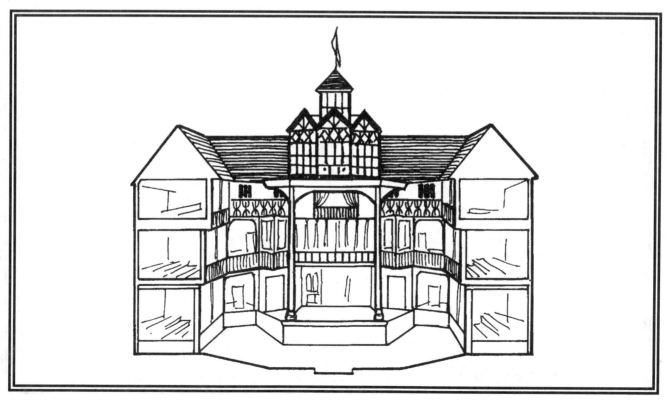

William Shakespeare *(cont.)*

James Audubon

James Audubon, born April 26, 1785, is noted for his beautiful paintings of birds in their natural habitats. Can you match each type of bird to its illustration? Write the correct letter before each number.

1. _____ blue jay

2. _____ owl

3. _____ crow

4. _____ sparrow

5. _____ hawk

6. _____ eagle

7. _____ woodpecker

8. _____ robin

9. _____ pigeon

10. _____ loon

Coretta Scott King

Coretta Scott King was born on April 28, 1927. She is the widow of the great civil rights leader, Dr. Martin Luther King, Jr., and she is also an activist in her own right. She continues to keep alive Dr. King's dream—that all people join together in love, peace, and acceptance.

As a class, read about the life of Mrs. King and learn what she does to further Dr. King's work. Then, answer the following question: ***What can you do to increase the love, peace, and acceptance in the world?***

_____

_____

_____

_____

_____

_____

_____

_____

_____

_____

_____

_____

_____

_____

_____

_____

_____

_____

Share your ideas with the class, and then choose something you can do together to make a peaceful difference in the world. Devise a plan for carrying out your choice, discuss your plan, and then sign a class agreement stating what each of you will do. Over time, continue to discuss your experiences and ideas.

April Showers Bring May Flowers

April is known for its rainy days that turn to the beautiful sunshine and flowers of spring. The students can create works of art that demonstrate this springtime change. Follow these directions:

Materials:

- old magazines
- 18" x 12" (45 cm x 30 cm) white paper
- rulers
- pencils
- scissors
- glue

Directions:

1. Let each student find a large picture of a rain scene and another picture (approximately the same size) of a springtime scene.

2. The two pictures should be trimmed to exactly the same size. The width of each picture should be an even measurement in inches or centimeters. For example, a good width would be 8 inches or 20 centimeters, but not 8 ³/₈ inches or 20.25 centimeters.

3. Measure the width and height of one picture.

4. Cut the white paper to the same height as the picture and cut it to double the width.

5. On the back of each picture, draw straight vertical lines ¹/₂ inch or 1 centimeter apart.

6. On the back of the white paper, draw straight vertical lines the same distance apart as on the pictures.

7. Accordion fold the white paper at the lines.

8. You will be cutting each of the two pictures into strips at the lines you have drawn. In order to keep the pictures in order, you will probably want to cut one strip at a time. Start with the far-left strip of the rain picture. Cut it off and then paste it to the far-left strip of the white paper.

9. Cut the far-left strip of the spring scene. Paste it in the next strip on the white paper.

10. Cut the next strip of the rain scene. Paste it. Follow it with the next of the spring scene and so on until the pictures are completely pasted, alternating rain and spring.

11. When complete, you should be able to look at the picture from one side and see the complete rain scene. From the other side you will see the complete spring scene. From the front, you will see the two intermingled.

12. If desired, paste the picture to a background (gluing only on the ridges so that the picture does not lie flat) and display it.

The Water Cycle

All of the water in the world is involved in the water cycle. This is how the cycle works:

1. **Evaporation:** The sun warms the water on the earth. Some of it is changed into a gas.

2. **Condensation**: Water vapor, the gas produced through evaporation, rises and forms clouds.

3. **Precipitation:** When the water vapor gets heavy, it falls back to the earth in various forms of precipitation. For example, if it is cold, it will snow; if it is warm, it will rain.

4. **Recycling:** Some precipitation is absorbed into the ground. The rest falls into streams, lakes, and oceans.

This cycle repeats endlessly. Do you think you know how it works? Well, here is another way to remember:

Water Cycle Rap

Raining here and raining there,
Raindrops falling everywhere.
Water Cycle, that's the name,
How it works, let me explain.
Condensation in the clouds,
Drops of rain fall to the ground.
Sun comes out, begins to beat
Upon the raindrops with its heat.
Dries up all the rain below,
Evaporation makes it so.
Up the vapor rises high,
Forming clouds up in the sky.
Water Cycle starts again,
Look outside, let's watch the rain.
— Karen Goldfluss

The Water Cycle

Water is constantly forming and circulating in a repeating pattern known as the water cycle. The steps in the water cycle are listed below, but they are out of order. Rewrite them correctly on the flow chart. Begin in the top circle.

- Some water is absorbed into the ground. The rest falls into streams, lakes, and oceans.
- The sun warms the water on the earth, and some of it is changed into a gas.
- When the water vapor gets heavy, it falls back to the earth in various forms.
- Water vapor rises and forms clouds.

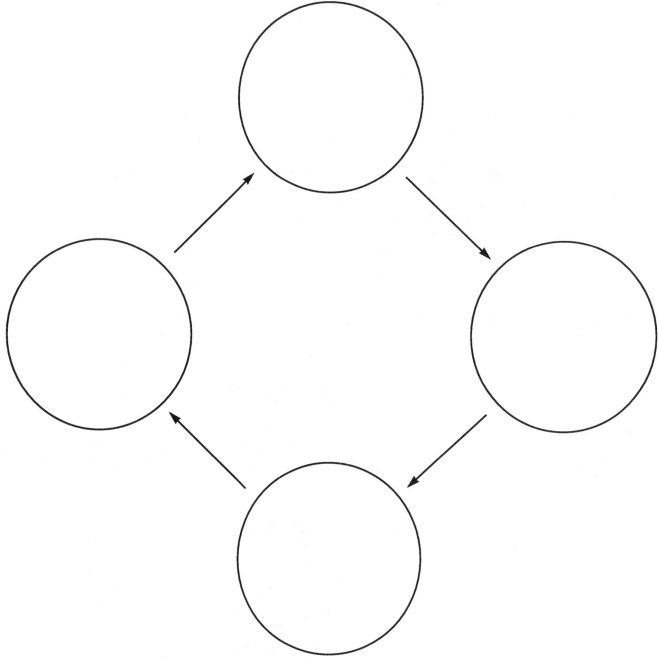

Teacher note: See page 5.

Shape Poem

A shape poem is a poem that is written in the form of a shape, and it also tells about whatever shape it takes. For example, the words of a shape poem about roller coasters might be written in up and down hills or loops.

Using the shape of the umbrella below, write a shape poem about rain or umbrellas.

All About Rain

In 10 minutes, how many things can you think of that are associated with rain? Ready, set, go!

Don't Forget Your Umbrella

Challenge your students to make a small umbrella without looking at one as a model.* It is likely to prove trickier than they might think.

Divide the students into teams of approximately three members each. Provide them with some or all of the following materials:

- plastic straws
- fabric
- scissors
- glue
- needles and thread

- tape
- construction paper
- wire hangers
- wire cutters

Give the students a set amount of time (whatever is appropriate for your class) and let them problem-solve together in order to come up with a reasonable design.

When all of the models are ready, let the students share theirs with the other teams. Also show a few manufactured umbrellas so that they can compare.

*Note: If it would benefit your students, you may wish to let them examine some manufactured umbrellas before or while they make their own.

String Art

String art is a method by which you can create a picture using colored string or thread, brads (small nails), and a board. You can be completely creative or follow a pattern, as in the example below.

Materials:

- any color embroidery thread
- wood board (approximately 8" x 6"/20 cm x 15 cm; painted if desired)
- 27 paper fasteners
- small hammer
- raindrop pattern
- tape

Directions:

1. Lay the pattern over the board and keep it in place with tape.

2. Nail in a brad through the pattern at each indicated dot. Be sure to leave about half of each brad sticking up.

3. Tie a length of embroidery thread to brad number 1.

4. Wrap the thread around each nail in succession, as shown. Tie it off at brad number 28 (1).

5. When complete, carefully tear away the pattern.

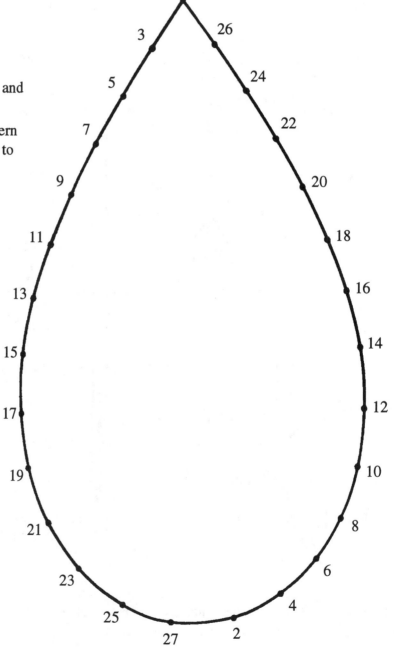

From Sprinkle to Squall

Each of the words on the right is a synonym for rain, but each word means a different kind of rain. Circle the correct word from each set of three for each definition.

Definition	Word		
1. a very light rain	drizzle	tempest	torrent
2. a violent rain	flow	shower	storm
3. a rapid, violent stream of water	flow	torrent	shower
4. a severe rain	flow	drizzle	tempest
5. an outpouring of rain	squall	flow	sprinkle
6. a great flood	squall	tempest	deluge
7. a brief fall of rain	storm	shower	gale
8. a sudden, violent wind and rain	squall	tempest	flood
9. a slight rain	sprinkle	deluge	storm
10. a drenching rain	sprinkle	downpour	squall

Rainy Day Puzzle

Each of the words in the word box is a different word for rain. Can you make a crossword for these words? You will need to lay the words out in a crossword grid.

Words having a letter in common can cross over one another, as in the illustration to the right.

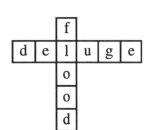

However, no two words can run side-by-side, as in the illustration to the right.

Once you have the words in place, make a crossword grid without the letters and write a clue for each word. Take your puzzle home and challenge your parents or older siblings.

Word Box

deluge	flood	sprinkle	thunderstorm
downpour	flow	squall	torrent
drizzle	rain	storm	
fall	shower	tempest	

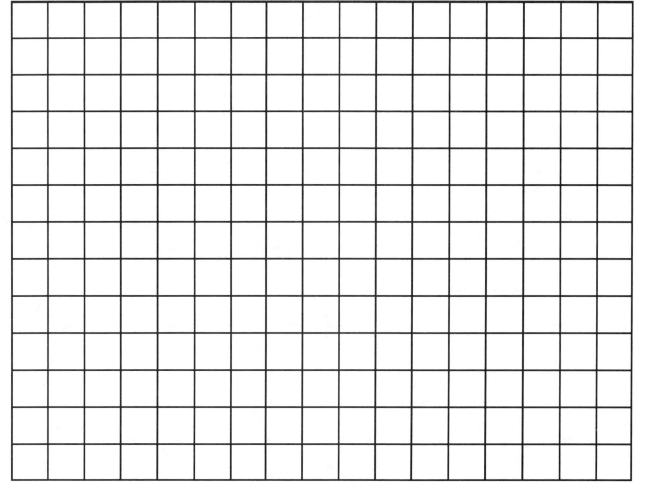

How Wet Is the World?

The wettest places in the world are in the Tropics because air is moist over the seas and where temperatures are high. The driest places are where winds blow over hot land or where a mountain range leaves a "rain shadow" on its leeward side. "Rainfall belts" move north and south with the sun; therefore, some places, such as Italy, have most of their rain in the winter, while others, such as China, have more in the summer. The map below indicates general rainfall around the world. Color the map and the key according to the information given and the patterns on the map.

Map Key
light snow (white)
seldom rainy (yellow)
light seasonal rain (green)
heavy seasonal rain (blue)
monthly rain (purple)

Rain Games

Here are three rainy day games to keep the whole class busy, thinking, and having a good time.

Rain Names

Divide the class into pairs. Set a timer for 10 minutes. Ask the pairs to list all the books, movies, and songs they can think of that have "rain" in their titles. At the end of the allotted time, count who has the most titles, and then award that pair two small prizes.

Rainy Day Charades

Brainstorm with your fellow teachers or your family members for book, movie, and song titles that have to do with rain in one way or another. (For example, "April Showers" is about rain while the movie, *Rain Man*, simply has the word rain in its title. Write these titles on small scraps of paper. On a rainy day, have the students come to the front of the class one at a time. Each will do a charade for a title that he or she draws from a hat.

To extend this, use titles that have to do with weather in general such as *Gone With the Wind*, *Greased Lightning*, and "You Are My Sunshine."

Bird Shower

Either individually, in teams, or as a class, have the students use their imaginations and humor to think of things they or nature can do in the rain that they cannot normally do otherwise. They can begin with the obvious, such as "get wet while walking home from school," but they should challenge themselves creatively as they progress, such as with "birds can take a shower" (hence, the name of the game).

Tic-Tac-Earth

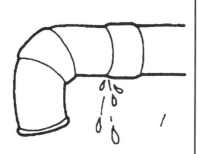

Find a water leak at home, at school, or in a business. Report it.

Snip each section of a six-pack ring before you throw it out.

Fill a large plastic jug with water and some pebbles for weight. Place it in the toilet tank. This will save water every time the toilet is flushed.

Next time you find a bug in your house or classroom, help it get back outside safely. Do not kill it!

Create your own ecology project—a newsletter, fund-raising event, play, or letter-writing campaign—to help others become ecologically aware.

Begin using a recycling box at home for paper. Place all recyclable paper there rather than throwing it out.

Construct an art project out of recycled bags and boxes.

Turn off the water while you brush your teeth. Turn it on only for rinsing.

Share something you have learned about ecology with your parent, teacher, or another adult you know.

Teacher note: See page 5.

Tic-Tac-Earth *(cont.)*

Keep a tally sheet of everything you throw away over one week.

Next time you shop with your parent at the grocery store, bring old paper or plastic bags. Use these to bag your groceries instead of new bags.

Write a crossword or wordsearch puzzle using ecology words you have learned. Give it to a friend or classmate to solve.

Make a bird feeder. Cut a grapefruit in half and eat the fruit. Fill the peel with bird seed and suet. Tie three pieces of string to the grapefruit and attach it to a tree branch.

Create your own ecology project—a newsletter, fund-raising event, play, or letter-writing campaign—to help others become ecologically aware.

Place a box at home for collecting glass and another for collecting plastic. Bring them to a recycling center when they are full.

Clean out your closet and cupboards. Donate the things you no longer need or want to a charitable organization.

Use only cloth towels and napkins for one week.

Turn off the lights when you are not using them.

Teacher note: See page 5.

Making Recycled Paper

The following recipe yields one sheet of recycled paper.

Materials:

- a newspaper
- water
- blender

- measuring cup
- flat wooden board (newspaper size)
- piece of window screen (cut to fit inside the pan)

- square pan

Directions:

1. Rip two or three pages from the newspaper into tiny pieces.

2. Place the paper in the blender and add 5 cups (1.2 L) of water. (In order to color the paper, you can use a natural dye. Add the dying agent to the water and paper before blending. You might try strawberries, tea, coffee, grated carrots, grapes, or any of several other fruits or plants that you think might color your paper.)

3. Blend until the paper is pulpy.

4. Pour 1" (2.5 cm) of water into the pan.

5. Place the screen in the pan.

6. Pour the water/paper mixture over the screen and spread it evenly.

7. Drain the water by lifting the screen.

8. Place the screen with the mixture on it inside a section of newspaper.

9. Flip the paper over so that the screen is on top of the mixture.

10. Place the board on top and press down to squeeze out the extra water.

11. Open the newspaper section and remove the screen.

12. Keep the newspaper open and let the mixture dry for at least one day.

13. When the mixture is dry, carefully peel it off the newspaper. Your paper is ready!

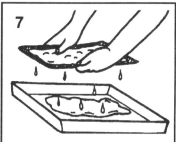

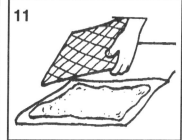
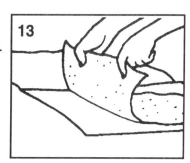

Ecology Survey

Ask yourself the following questions. Afterwards, add your answers together with the rest of the class to take a whole-class survey.

1. I use both sides of my paper.

   ❑ yes   ❑ no

2. I reuse paper bags and glass and plastic containers.

   ❑ yes   ❑ no

3. I turn off the water while brushing my teeth.

   ❑ yes   ❑ no

4. I pick up litter when I see it, even if it is not mine.

   ❑ yes   ❑ no

5. I take short showers instead of baths.

   ❑ yes   ❑ no

6. I turn off lights, televisions, and so forth, when I am the last to leave a room.

   ❑ yes   ❑ no

7. I wear a sweater when it is cold instead of turning the heat up.

   ❑ yes   ❑ no

8. I use a cloth or sponge instead of paper towels in order to wipe up spills.

   ❑ yes   ❑ no

9. I walk, ride my bike, or take a bus instead of asking someone to drive me.

   ❑ yes   ❑ no

10. I recycle newspapers, glass, aluminum, and plastic.

    ❑ yes   ❑ no

11. I throw litter in the proper containers.

    ❑ yes   ❑ no

12. I donate old clothes and toys to charitable groups rather than throw them away.

    ❑ yes   ❑ no

13. I cut six-pack rings before throwing them away, so they will not pose a threat to marine life.

    ❑ yes   ❑ no

14. I think about what I want before I open the refrigerator door, so it can be closed again quickly.

    ❑ yes   ❑ no

15. I buy products that use minimal packaging instead of those that are over-packaged.

    ❑ yes   ❑ no

Making a Composter

A key to composting, which is the speeded process of naturally decomposing organic materials, is the circulation of air. Moisture, temperature, and bacterial presence are also factors. To compost is as simple as piling leaves and mowed grass in an outside corner and regularly stirring and turning the compost heap to speed its decomposition. A composter can also be as structured as the following.

Note: This activity uses sharp instruments and should only be done by adults or with strict adult supervision.

Materials:

- three 2-liter plastic bottles
- clear tape
- mesh netting
- needle
- rubber band
- hot water
- sharp knife or razor
- marking pen that writes on plastic

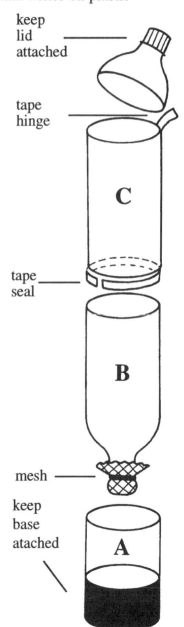

Directions:

1. If the bottles have plastic bases, fill two of the bottles halfway with hot water. Cap the bottles and swirl the water until the heat-sensitive glue attaching the bases softens enough so that the bases can be removed. Also do this to remove any labels from the bottles.

2. If the bases are not removable, mark cutting lines and cut with the knife as follows:

   a. Cut off the top portion of Bottle A where it begins to taper. Leave the base. Save the top.

   b. Cut off the base of Bottle B where it begins to taper. Recycle the base.

   c. Cut off the base and top of Bottle C where they begin to taper. Recycle the base and the top.

3. With the needle, punch several air holes in Bottles B and C and the top portion of Bottle A. Heat the needle first in a candle flame if necessary. This will make it easier to poke through the plastic.

4. Keep the cap on Bottle Top A. Place mesh netting over the top of Bottle B and fasten around the rim with the rubber band.

5. Construct a column as illustrated, attaching Bottle Top A (point up) to Bottle C (now a cylinder) with a piece of tape on one side to act as a hinge. Attach Bottle C on top of Bottle B so that their circular openings meet. Tape them together all the way around. Place Bottle B point down in Bottle A so that its netted top is within the cylinder of Bottle A. Bottle A should still have its base. This is the bottom of the composter into which liquid will drain.

6. Organic materials (such as leaves, grass, and organic household garbage) can now be placed in the composter through the hinged opening between Bottle Top A and Bottle C. All this composted material will become rich, fertile soil for your yard or garden.

The Art of Recycling

Recycle the following materials into works of art.

1. **Soda pop can tabs**

   necklaces

   collage

2. **Juice can**

   pencil holder (Cover with yarn or fabric and decorate.)

3. **Wood cubes and shavings**

   game markers or dice

   paint just for fun

   hair on 3-D works of art

   collage

4. **Plastic spoon**

   stick puppet (Add yarn hair, clothes, and a face.)

5. **Margarine tub**

   planting pot

   keepsake holder (Cover with yarn or fabric and decorate.)

6. **Paper bags**

   puppets

   Halloween jack-o-lanterns (Stuff with paper, tying the top together to make a stem, and paint it.)

   costumes

7. **Newspaper**

   dolls (Crumple a piece to make a round head, roll another into a body shape, roll and fold others for arms and legs, tape or tie the pieces together, paint, and add yarn for hair.)

8. **Straws**

   frames

9. **Plastic produce containers**

   weaving

   plaster of Paris handprints

   paint

10. **Magazines**

    collages

    mosaics (Tear small pieces in different colors and use in place of beads, stones, or sand.)

    beads (Tear strips, roll around a pencil, and glue. When dry, string them on yarn or dental floss.)

Rock Candy

Here is a tasty way to enjoy the "earth."

Materials:

- measuring cup
- large saucepan or pot
- spoon
- baby food jars
- pencils
- 4" (10 cm) length soft cord (one per student)

Ingredients:

- 8 cups (2 L) water
- 16 cups (4 L) sugar

Directions:

1. To prepare the jars, have each student tie a string around the center of a pencil, allowing half of the full length to hang down from the pencil. Balance the pencil on the rim of the baby food jar and set it aside.

2. Heat the water over a medium heat.

3. Add the sugar, one cup (250 mL) at a time, waiting until each portion has dissolved before adding next cup. Continue until no more sugar dissolves.

4. Remove the pot from the stove and cool until warm.

5. Pour the sugar mixture into the jars around the string and pencils. Set the jars aside again. Within a few hours, crystals will begin to form. Leave the jars overnight.

6. Pull the candy string out of the liquid in the jar and enjoy it!

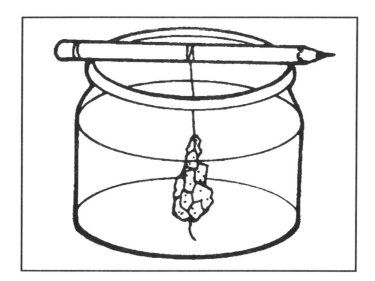

Note: If you pour the remaining sugar liquid from all the jars back into the pot, reboil, and proceed with the fifth step again, the candy rock string will grow even larger.

Write On for Our Earth

Teacher Note: See page 5.

1. Imagine you have discovered a new planet where people can live. Make a list of guidelines for people to follow to prevent the new planet from becoming polluted.

2. Write a letter from the point of view of an endangered species convincing people to protect them.

3. Write about what the world might be like 50 years from now if people continue to treat it badly.

4. Write about what the world might be like 50 years from now if people treat it with respect and care.

5. Make up a chant about the earth and how we can help it. Teach the chant to the rest of the class and chant it in an Earth Day parade or demonstration.

6. Write new words for a familiar song so that it is about the environment and protecting and loving the earth.

7. Write and draw a comic strip about our planet.

8. Write catchy slogans for posters and advertisements about Earth Day.

9. Write and perform a special newscast that tells about the problems our planet is facing and how people can help.

10. Take an object that people would consider trash (milk carton, egg carton, paper towel tube, broken toy, etc.) and list at least 10 new uses for it.

11. Write a letter to an environmental organization to find out what you can do to help.

Greenpeace
1436 U Street NW
Washington, D.C. 20009

Sierra Club
730 Polk Street
San Francisco, CA 94009

World Wildlife Fund
1250 24th Street NW
Washington, D.C. 20037

Oceanic Society
218 D Street SE
Washington, D.C. 20003

National Audubon Society
645 Pennsylvania Avenue SE
Washington, D.C. 20003

Rainforest Action Network
450 Sansome St., Suite 700
San Francisco, CA 94111

Rain Forest Word Game

All of the following puzzle answers are products we get from the rain forest and its raw materials. To find out what they are, fill in the blank above each letter with the letter that comes before it in the alphabet.

1. _ _ _ _ _ _ _ _ _
    D I F X J O H H V N

2. _ _ _ _ _ _ _ _
    N B S H B S J O F

3. _ _ _ _
    T P B Q

4. _ _ _ _ _ _
    D B O E M F T

5. _ _ _ _ _ _ _
    T O F B L F S T

6. _ _ _ _ _ _ _ _
    N F E J D J O F T

7. _ _ _ _ _ _
    C B O B O B T

8. _ _ _ _ _ _ _
    B W P D B E P T

9. _ _ _ _ _ _ _
    D J O O B N P O

10. _ _ _ _ _ _
    W B O J M M B

11. _ _ _ _ _
    D I J M J

12. _ _ _ _ _ _
    S V C C F S

13. _ _ _ _ _ _ _ _ _
    N B Z P O O B J T F

14. _ _ _ _
    S J D F

15. _ _ _ _ _ _
    D V S B S F

Leaf Through It

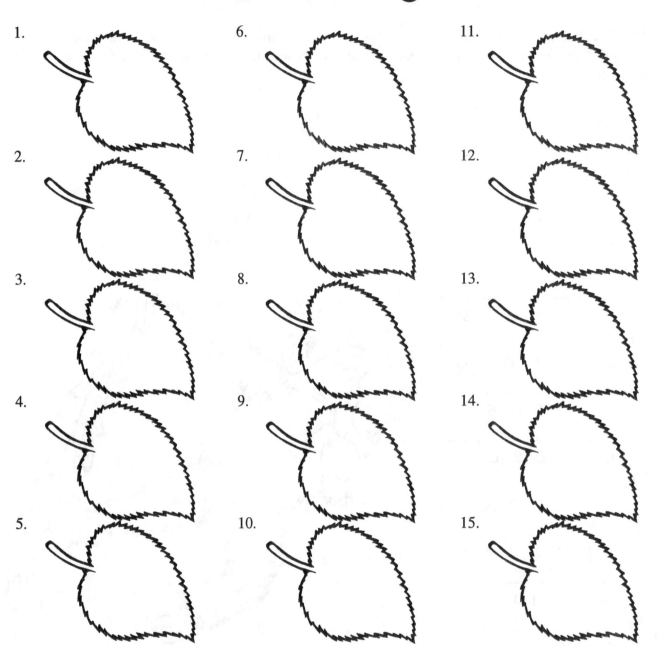

1.

2.

3.

4.

5.

6.

7.

8.

9.

10.

11.

12.

13.

14.

15.

Fold under before copying.

Answer Key

1.

2.

3.

4.

5.

6.

7.

8.

9.

10.

11.

12.

13.

14.

15.

Under the Umbrella

1.
2.
3.
4.
5.
6.
7.
8.
9.
10.

Fold under before copying.

Answer Key

1.	4.	7.	9.
2.	5.	8.	10.
3.	6.		

Open Worksheet Skills

The open worksheet pages are ready to use. Simply fill in the directions and write the skill you want to reinforce. Make a copy for each student or pair of students or glue the worksheet to tagboard and laminate. Place the laminated copy at an appropriate classroom center along with water-based pens that can be easily wiped off for reuse.

Ideas and references for using these worksheets are provided below.

Math: facts, decimals, word problems, place value, sets, money problems, measurement, percent, multiplication, division, standard and metric conversions, basic geometry

Language: abbreviations, contractions, compound words, prefixes, suffixes, rhymes, plurals, anagrams, synonyms, antonyms, homonyms

> **Abbreviations:** names of states/provinces, days of the week, units of measurement, months of the year, road markers (street, avenue, boulevard, etc.), titles (Mister, Doctor, Governor, etc.)

> **Prefixes:** dis-, sub-, con-, un-, over-, uni-, re-, a-, retro-, anti-, di-, be-, bi-, ex-, inter-, mis-, super-, para-, non-, post-, pre-, neo-

> **Suffixes:** -able, -cy, -ine, -hood, -ology, -ful, -ive, -less, -ly, -en, -some, -ee, -ance, -cian, -et, -oid, -ward, -ness, -ile, -ous, -dom, -fy, -ice, -tude, -ure, -ism, -ite, -ist, -ade, -ese

> **Plurals:** -s, -es, -ies

> **Anagrams:** dear, dare, read; notes, stone, tones; fowl, flow, wolf; veil, vile, evil; tea, ate, eat; shoe, hoes, hose; vase, save; pea, ape; north, thorn; flea, leaf; veto, vote; cone, once; stop, tops. pots, post, spot, steam, meats, mates, tames

> **Homonyms:** eight, ate; whole, hole; red, read; hour, our; peace, piece; pare, pair; lone, loan; pale, pail; knew, new, gnu; nose, knows; blew, blue; would, wood; for, four, fore; by, bye, buy; sense, cents, scents; two, too, to; sun, son

Social Studies: countries, continents, capitals, ports, lakes, oceans, rivers, leaders, founders, famous people

April Record Form

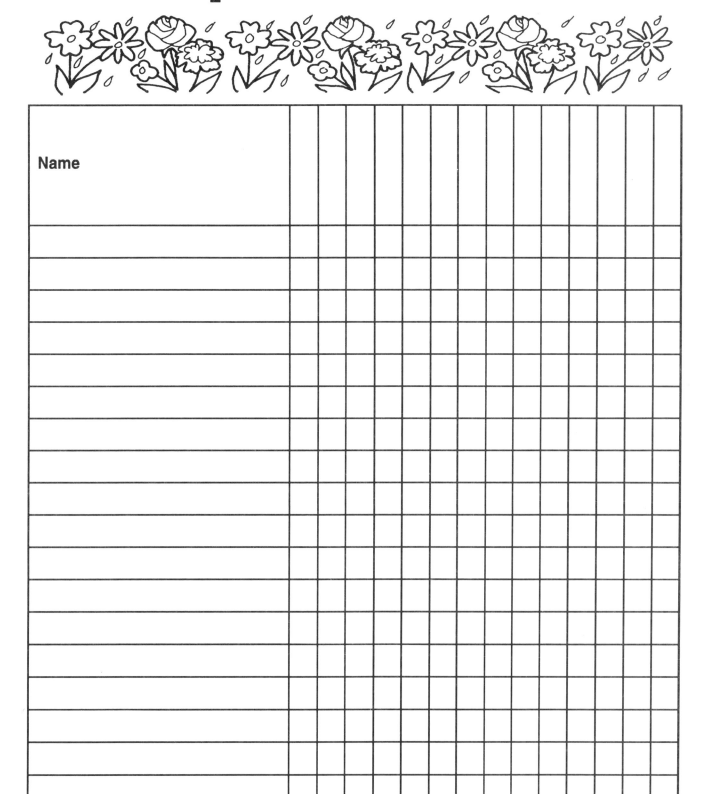

Name												

Invitation and Thank You

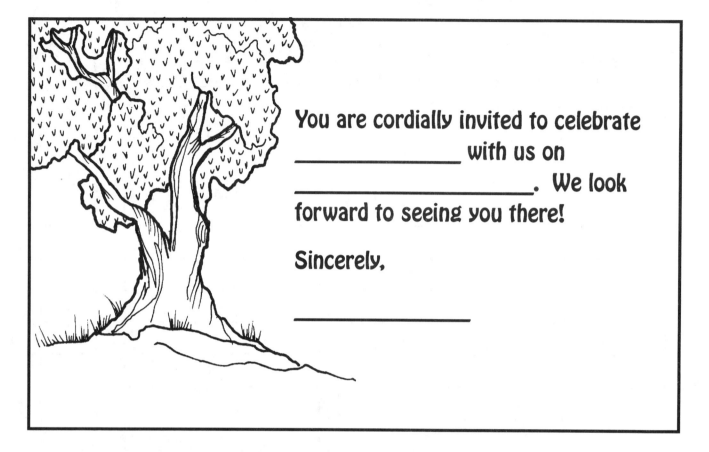

You are cordially invited to celebrate _____ with us on _____. We look forward to seeing you there!

Sincerely,

_____

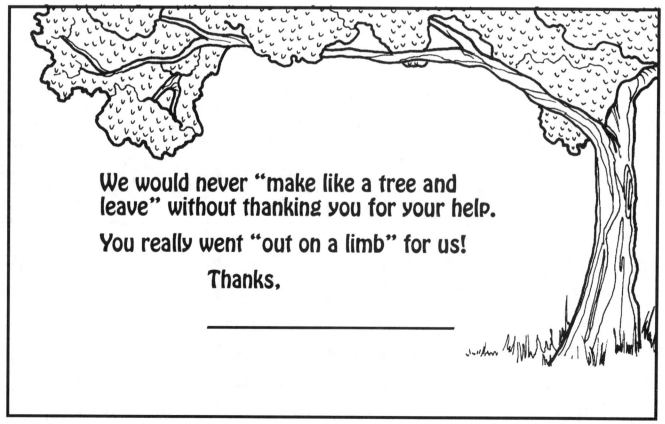

We would never "make like a tree and leave" without thanking you for your help.

You really went "out on a limb" for us!

Thanks,

_____

Contract and Award

My Behavior Contract

I will try my best to turn the showers to flowers.

I will not _____.

I will _____.

For my new behavior, I will receive _____.

_____
Signed

_____
Teacher

_____
Date

Award

_____

*has demonstrated a love
of our earth by*

_____

_____

Teacher signature

_____

Date

April News

70

Dear Parents and Guardians,

Soon we will be doing some special projects that correspond to the month of April. In order to complete our projects and make the most of the experience, we would like to ask your help in collecting the following items: _____

_____

We can also use your help in the classroom on _____ at _____.

If you are able to help, please send the notice below with your child to me.

With many thanks from our classroom,

_____

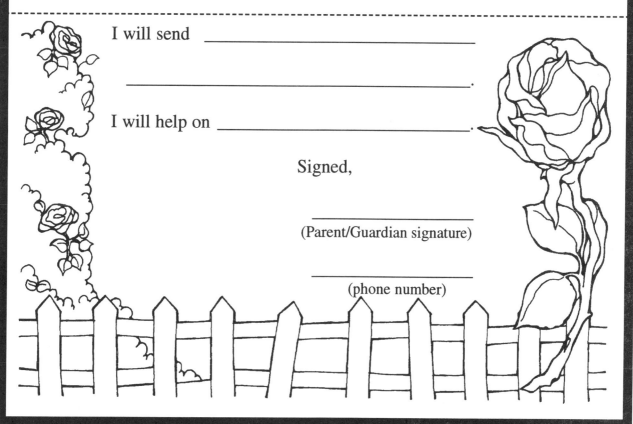

I will send _____

_____.

I will help on _____.

Signed,

_____
(Parent/Guardian signature)

_____
(phone number)

Clip Art

Clip Art *(cont.)*

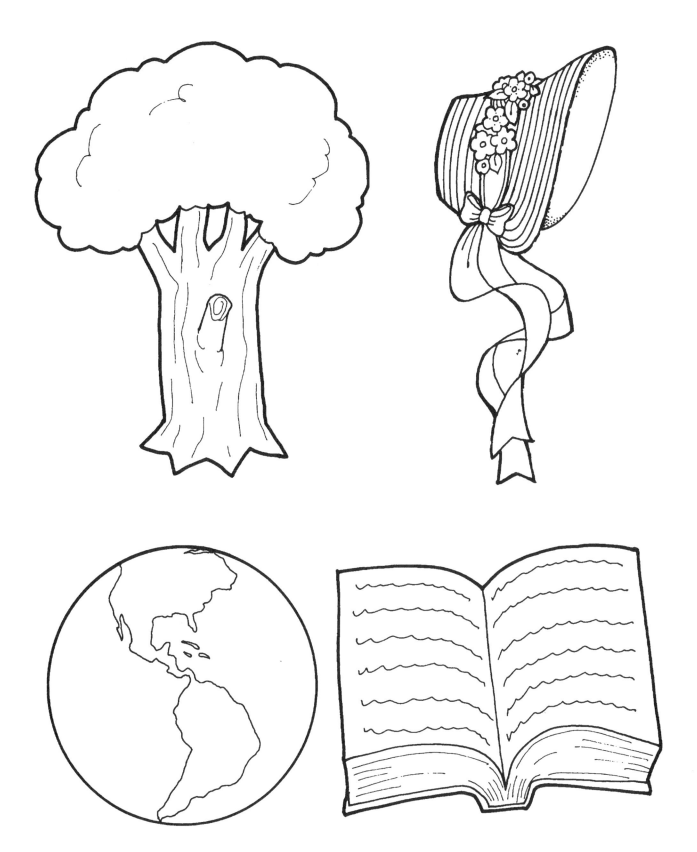

Dear _____,

_____

_____

_____

_____

_____

_____

_____

_____

_____

_____

_____

_____

_____

_____

_____

_____

_____

_____

Bookmarks

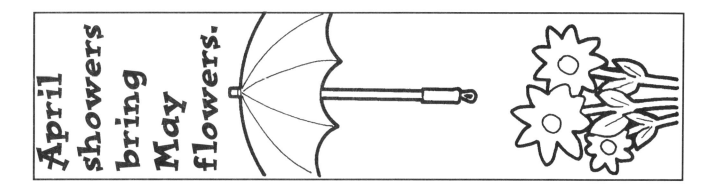

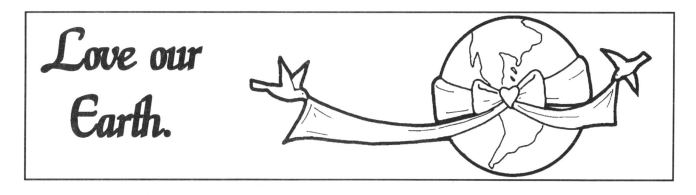

Bulletin Board

April brings both Arbor Day and Earth Day, so this is a good month to focus on respect and care for the earth. Brainstorm with the students for ways that they as a class can make a difference. Choose some projects together that the class would like to commit to for a period of time. As they work on the projects, photograph them in action. Also collect their writings and art projects that deal with the care of the earth.

Once these materials have been gathered, create a bulletin board display as a class. Use the patterns on the following pages to title and illustrate the board. Color in the patterns in a way that reflects the nature of your bulletin board display.

Alternative: Make a board that will not only impact the students but visitors to your classroom as well. Over a period of one week, have the students save and bring in all the junk mail they and their parents receive at home. Staple all this mail to the bulletin board under the message "Let's Stop the Waste!"

Bulletin Board (cont.)

Bulletin Board (cont.)

Bulletin Board *(cont.)*

Answer Key

Page 12

roasted lamb bone = sacrifice of the first Passover
hard-boiled egg = new life
celery/parsley = spring
bitter herb (horseradish) = slavery
charoset (apples, nuts, wine, sugar, and cinnamon) = mortar used by Jews to build Egyptian cities

Page 16

1. face on sun
2. sunglasses on sun
3. flying cat
4. flying saucer
5. daytime stars
6. cherry topping on mountain
7. chimney on rail car
8. fish in rail car
9. tires on rail car
10. chicken on street
11. chicken on unicycle
12. one lens on glasses
13. running shoes with suit
14. mop for hair
15. candy cane buggy handles
16. door on buggy
17. rockers on buggy
18. frog feet in buggy
19. shark fin in gutter
20. wrist watch on dog
21. man crawling
22. leash and collar on man
23. upright dog walking a man

Page 31

1. exerciser
2. wonderful you
3. I love you, too.
4. You are great.
5. speedy one
6. light and easy

Page 36

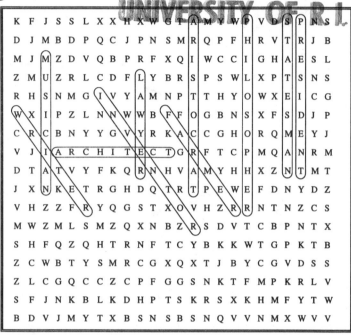

architect, aristocrat, farmer, inventor, lawyer, musician, philosopher, president, statesman, and writer

Page 42

1. e
2. i
3. h
4. j
5. a
6. g
7. f
8. c
9. b
10. d

Page 51

1. drizzle
2. storm
3. torrent
4. tempest
5. flow
6. deluge
7. shower
8. squall
9. sprinkle
10. downpour

Page 63

1. chewing gum
2. margarine
3. soap
4. candles
5. sneakers
6. medicines
7. bananas
8. avocados
9. cinnamon
10. vanilla
11. chili
12. rubber
13. mayonnaise
14. rice
15. curare